OCS Study
MMS 2003-065

Coastal Marine Institute

Preparation of an Interactive Key for Northern Gulf of Mexico Polychaete Taxonomy Employing the DELTA/INTKEY System

I0439716

Final Report

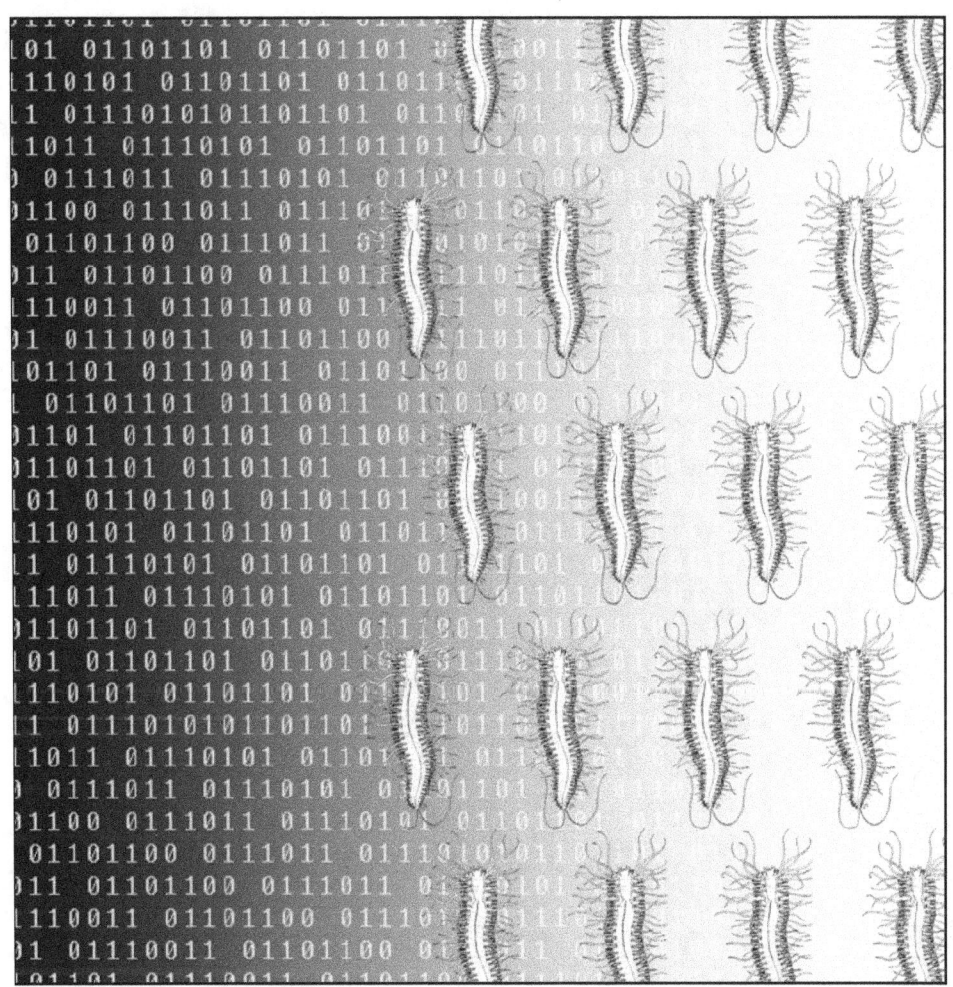

U.S. Department of the Interior
Minerals Management Service
Gulf of Mexico OCS Region

Cooperative Agreement
Coastal Marine Institute
Louisiana State University

OCS Study
MMS 2003-065

Coastal Marine Institute

Preparation of an Interactive Key for Northern Gulf of Mexico Polychaete Taxonomy Employing the DELTA/INTKEY System

Final Report

Author

R.S. Carney

October 2003

Prepared under MMS Contract
14-35-0001-30951-16801
by
Louisiana State University
Baton Rouge, Louisiana 70803

Published by

U.S. Department of the Interior
Minerals Management Service
Gulf of Mexico OCS Region

Cooperative Agreement
Coastal Marine Institute
Louisiana State University

DISCLAIMER

This report was prepared under contract between the Minerals Management Service (MMS) and Louisiana State University. This report has been technically reviewed by the MMS and approved for publication. Approval does not signify that the contents necessarily reflect the views and policies of the Service, nor does mention of trade names or commercial products constitute endorsement or recommendation for use. It is, however, exempt from review and compliance with MMS editorial standards.

REPORT AVAILABILITY

Extra copies of the report may be obtained from the Public Information Office (Mail Stop 5034) at the following address:

U.S. Department of the Interior
Minerals Management Service
Gulf of Mexico OCS Region
Public Information Office (MS 5034)
1201 Elmwood Park Boulevard
New Orleans, Louisiana 70123-2394
Telephone Number: 1-800-200-GULF or (504) 736-2519

CITATION

Suggested Citation:

Carney, R.S. 2003. Preparation of an interactive key for the northern Gulf of Mexico polychaete taxonomy employing the DELTA/INTKEY system. U.S. Dept. of the Interior, Minerals Management Service, Gulf of Mexico OCS, New Orleans, La. OCS Study MMS 2003-065, 38 pp.

SUMMARY

The seafloor subject to disturbance by outer continental oil and gas activity is home to a few thousand species. Surveys of the seafloor undertaken to make informed decisions about future development and monitoring undertaken to assure acceptable levels of impact from existing activity are heavily dependent upon sampling and correctly identifying a large fraction of that diverse fauna. Assuring correct and consistent identification of species is a difficult problem. The task requires a tremendous breadth of expertise. There is a decreasing pool of experts, and taxonomic data are not now handled and synthesized in a manner that facilitates identification. Resource management agencies such as the Minerals Management Service have made noteworthy efforts to improve taxonomic quality such as production of comprehensive faunal keys and maintainence of voucher collections. These efforts, however, have not overcome the ecological and taxonomic communities' historical lack of a focused effort to improve identification.

Over the past twenty years, taxonomy has innovatively incorporated computer database methodology into the management, analysis, and synthesis of taxonomic data. As a result, there is a transition underway in which traditional taxonomic papers, monographs, and identification keys are being replaced by interactive data-management systems. Part of this transition has been the development of Computer Aided Taxonomic Identification (CATI). CATI is now sufficiently mature that its methods of taxonomic data analysis should be adopted by agencies supporting species identification.

As a demonstration project, the information on northern Gulf of Mexico polychaete worms was converted into a database and interactive key. The Descriptive Language for Taxonomy (DELTA) (Dallwitz 1980; Dallwitz et al. 1993, 1995, 1999, 2000) was used to develop the database and a companion program INTKEY (Dallwitz 1980; Dallwitz et al. 1993, 1995, 2000) used to develop the interactive key. The exercise proved the practicality of basing taxonomic QA/QC efforts upon CATI.

TABLE OF CONTENTS

LIST OF FIGURES

LIST OF TABLES

1. Introduction

1.1 Intent and Content

This report is intended as an introduction to Computer Aided Taxonomic Identification (CATI) for ecologists and ocean resource managers for whom correct and consistent identification of organisms is an important aspect of environmental surveying and monitoring. As a demonstration of CATI's utility, DELTA, a Descriptive Language for Taxonomy (Dallwitz 1980; Dallwitz et al. 1993, 1995, 1999, 2000) was used to convert traditional taxonomic information on polychaete worms into an interactive key to be used with the program INTKEY (Dallwitz 1980; Dallwitz et al. 1993, 1995, 2000). This report provides a brief introduction to CATI in the general terms of database management. It is explained how CATI occupies a common ground meeting the needs of taxonomic analysis and the ecological need for identification. The DELTA system is explained and a guide to the DELTA literature provided. The process of building the polychaete database is explained and the files provided with the database detailed. Use of the interactive key and INTKEY is explained.

DELTA and INTKEY are intended to run under Microsoft Windows operating system 95 and later. During this project, Windows 95, 98, Me, 2000 and 2000-Pro were used without difficulty. Use of DELTA, INTKEY, and the polychaete interactive key requires that the following steps be completed.

1. INTKEY and/or the entire DELTA system must be downloaded from: http://biodiversity.uno.edu/delta/www/programs.htm. The software comes as a self-extracting compressed file for the Windows (95, Me, 2000, and XP) operating system. An installation wizard leads the user through installation.

2. Gulf_Polychaetes must be downloaded from: http://biodiversity.bio.uno.edu/delta/www/data.htm. The downloaded folder contains a zip-compressed archive of 12 files and a folder of images in jpg and bitmapped format.

3. The user guides for DELTA and INTKEY that come with the software should be read and understood.

4. The Gulf polychaete interactive key can be run by double clicking on the file .../Gulf_Polychates/intkey.ink. Depending upon the installation INTKEY, the program will run directly or the user will be prompted to find the program INTKEY5.exe.

Note: The DELTA system is distributed with restrictions that include license fees and required citation (see Appendix 1). This study was done in full compliance with those restrictions. Users of the polychaete database reported herein must also comply.

It is important that DELTA, INTKEY, and polychaete database files be obtained on line. Both the programs and database are subject to revision by the participants of this study and any worker who finds errors or seeks to improve the database. Notification concerning errors and improvement should be addressed to Robert S. Carney, Coastal Ecology Institute, Louisiana State University, rcarne1@lsu.edu.

1.2 Changing Strategy for Taxonomic Quality Assurance

Inventories of fauna have been a data type of central importance to the management of the outer continental shelf since Gulf of Mexico baseline surveys were initiated in 1975 (Carney 1996) and impact assessment initiated in 1982 (Carney 1987). Without some form of faunal inventory it is impossible to answer the most fundamental management question, is there a deleterious ecological impact? Therefore, it is appropriate that management agencies such as the Minerals Management Service (MMS) assure the quality of these inventories in the sense of correct and consistent identification of organisms. Noteworthy efforts to improve the quality of inventories have been MMS' long term support of voucher collections at the US National Museum of Natural History, production of a seven volume taxonomic guide to the polychaetes of the Gulf of Mexico (Uebelacker and Johnson 1984) and the 14 volume taxonomic atlas of the Santa Maria Basin and western Santa Barbara Channel (Blake 1994). That report has been reissued by the Santa Barbara County Museum of Natural History as a commercially available series of guides (Scott and Blake 1997) and the traditional dichotomous keys are being made available via the world-wide ewb (http://www.sbnature.org/atlasweb/).

Even with good and well-used taxonomic guides, the task of correctly identifying the thousands of species collected in OCS habitats is increasingly difficult. Contrary to popular belief, many invertebrate species in familiar habitats are undescribed, and new studies in deepwater are encountering many more undescribed species. The need for increased species identification and taxonomic quality assurance is increasing at the same time that the availability of taxonomic expertise is declining.

MMS and other mission agencies continue to improve taxonomic quality assurance and quality control (QA/QC). Such efforts would benefit from the view that taxonomy is a form of data management. The types of data management adopted for taxonomic QA/QC must accomplish three important functions:

1. Facilitate correct and consistent identification of specimens independent of the identifier.

2. Allow for rapid incorporation of new taxa into identification system.

3. Allow for rapid improvement of identification as new characters are recognized and old characters are re-evaluated.

1.3 Understanding the Taxonomic QA/QC Problem

In order to understand the role that mission agencies play in assuring taxonomic quality, it is helpful to consider the general relationship between a mission agency and supportive sciences. MMS serves as a useful example. In order to answer the fundamental question whether unacceptable ecological damage occurs due to OCS activities, MMS depends upon many disciplines. Physical oceanography, chemical oceanography, geological oceanography, and benthic ecology (viewed as a part of biological oceanography) play important roles. Independent of MMS's needs, each of these disciplines has a vested interest in maintaining a high level of quality assurance and quality control (QA/QC) in the methods and technologies they apply. Most of often QA/QC is initiated by the peer community due to the increasing technical sophistication of the oceanographic questions being asked. When a research community imposes its own QA/QC requirements, the task of developing mission-specific requirements is made much easier for mission agencies.

Peer community-imposed QA/QC has best been developed in chemical and physical oceanography, highly quantitative fields. It is least developed in geological oceanography and benthic ecology, fields with a tradition of description and subjective interpretation. For benthic surveying formal QA/QC concerns most often address methodology problems of quantitative sampling and statistical problems of design, replication, and incorrect inference. Unfortunately, means of assuring quality of species identification are ad hoc from one research group to another.

If benthic ecologists provide only ad hoc QA/QC programs, why has the underlying discipline of taxonomy not addressed this need? Historically, the answer can be found in the following quotation.

> **"... it is not the job of the taxonomist to undertake the routine identification of ecological collections...Such identification is the responsibility of the ecologist...who wants the material identified. Nothing reduces the productivity of a research museum more than attempting to fill miscellaneous identification demands of the public. "**

Mayr and Ashlock 1991, p.338-339.

This sentiment expressed by Ernst Mayr, one of the most influential American systematists, has been prevalent in taxonomy. Correct and consistent identification is the obligation of the ecologists and those agencies dependent upon ecological data.

1.4 Overcoming the Taxonomic QA/QC Problem

Fortunately for all concerned about taxonomic QA/QC a common ground has emerged that serves the interest of the systematists studying phyletic relationships and the ecologist in need of a correct identification. That common ground is the use of computer databases. A database recording the traits of various taxa may be used for phyletic analysis (basic taxonomic research) and for computer aided identification (CATI).

Implementation of CATI has already begun within two marine invertebrate groups, crustaceans and polychaetes. Crustacea.Net (www.crustacea.net) is an international effort hosted at the Australian Museum in Sydney. It has already produced extremely useful interactive keys to higher taxa (Lowry 1999 onwards), amphipod families (Lowry and Springthorpe 2000 onwards), and stomatopods (Ahyong and Lowry, 2001). Dr. Robin Wilson of the Museum of Victoria and Dr. Pat Hutchings, of the Australian Museum are directing a program producing computer interactive keys of the polychaetes (http://www.museum.vic.gov.au/poly).

2. An Overview of Traditional Identification

2.1 The Identification Process: Discrimination and Naming

A discussion of the features of computer aided taxonomic identification is best begun with a brief discussion of traditional methods. From one perspective marine invertebrates are relatively easy to work with. A conscientious worker familiar with general invertebrate anatomy can very effectively discriminate one morphology from others and sort a mix of specimens into anatomically consistent groups given good specimens, good microscopes, and adequate time. Work speed and fidelity of allocation into consistent groups greatly improves with experience, but beyond experience a high degree taxonomic expertise is not really needed. From a second perspective, marine invertebrates are exceptionally hard to work with. The morphologies of marine invertebrates are extremely varied; so much so that experts in some taxa devote their professional lives to a single family. It is exceedingly hard for the non-expert to correctly identify a group of anatomically similar specimens to species. Correct identification may require a very high level of expertise in taxonomy. In short, identification is much harder than discrimination.

2.2 Does Management Need Species Identification?

Does management need both discrimination and identification to species? This is a complex question and no simple answer can be given at this time. The most practical answer is a two part "yes". Part one deals with taxonomic resolution of discrimination; surveys and monitoring need to be carried out at the species level even if the species groups are not identified. Ecological theory views species and their populations as the most important groups interacting with the environment. Applied studies must be linked to the best and most contemporary science, species-level ecology. Part two deals with identification of the species. Without correct species identification, every survey and monitoring project becomes a stand-alone task. No syntheses about the nature of faunal variation in space and time can be confidently developed, and it is impossible to bring the full weight of past evidence to bear on a question such as whether oil and gas activities cause unacceptable environmental damage.

2.3 Taxonomy as Data Management

Data gathering in taxonomy is the observation of specimens, recognition of traits, assessment of those traits, and compilation of the relationships between traits and organisms. Recognition of informative traits is the hardest intellectual part of this process. New technologies are always allowing new traits to be recognized, and new traits challenge previous taxonomies. In effect, taxonomists are constantly maintaining and revising a data matrix (Figure 2-1). Each row in the matrix is a taxon (species, higher, or lower) and each column a character (trait). The characters are of many types and can have various different states. Every time a new taxon is added, the relationship among taxa and characters may change, new characters may emerge, or new character states. The matrix may be quite large and difficult to use.

4

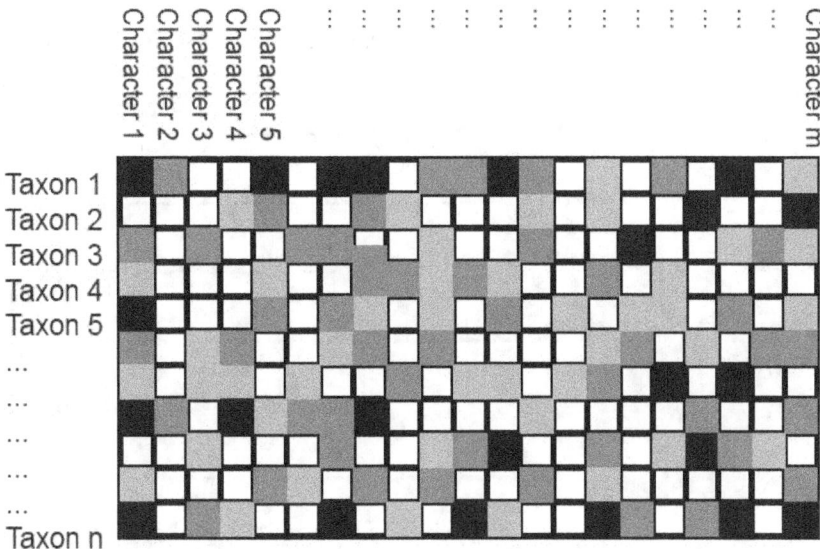

Figure 2-1 Taxa-Character matrix representation of taxonomic data.

Dichotomous keys are the most familiar tool of species identification. They allow identification of a species by answering a series of questions in the form of a couplet. Each answer leads to another question until the species is identified. Keys are written by experts for use by non-experts. Some are famous and some are infamous in the sense of being confusing, hard to use, and containing errors. Whatever the evaluation of the end user, dichotomous keys represent considerable thought on the part of the author, as they try and reduce the level of knowledge needed by the non-expert to make a correct and consistent identification. The process of making a useful key is best understood in the larger context of taxonomic information management.

Conceptually, identification of a species using the information in the Taxa-Character matrix is simple. The matrix just needs to be partitioned by examining the character states that match those of an unknown specimen. The partitioning can take the form of a series of questions, beginning with any character. This is illustrated in Figure 2-2. The hypothetical unknown organism shows state four of character one. All taxa with that same state are retained as possible candidates, all other eliminated. A second, third, and so on question can be asked until a single match remains. This process is termed random entry examination. The user is free to start with any character, and each question deals only with a single character. Implementation of random entry identification has been difficult for three reasons: 1) Data management - requires easy access to a potentially large and complex matrix. 2) Expertise - the large number of characters requires a high level of expertise to use. 3) Prematurity - the compiler of the matrix may feel that it is too tentative for use by non-experts.

Query 0 - WHERE Characters 1,5,7,& 20 have states 4,2,2,1,3 or otherwise.

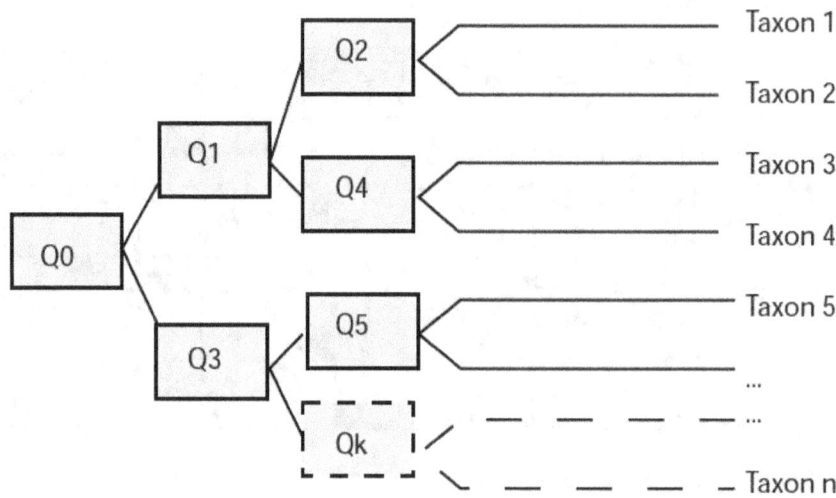

Figure 2-2 Generalized dichotomous keys are a hierachical tree of questions, Qn.

Query - WHERE Character 1 equals state 4?

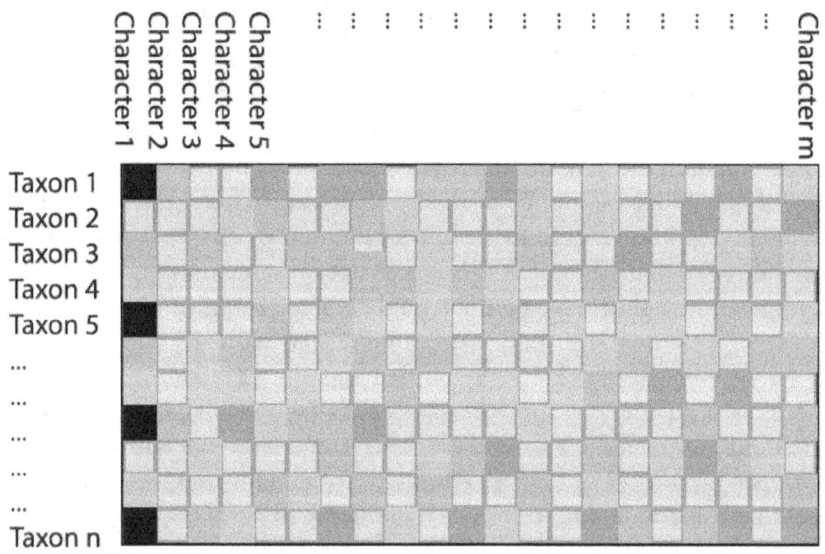

Figure 2-3 Querying a taxa-character matrix seeks matches in any state.

Traditionally, experts have overcome the impracticality of querying the entire taxon character matrix by producing a dichotomous key. The expert studies the whole complex matrix and then develops a series of simpler couples (questions with only two answers). These questions completely partition the matrix allowing each taxon in it to be identified. This process is shown diagrammatically in figure 2.2. Each question should be simple, but often are confusing and include many characters and specific character traits. An fixed sequence of questions must be answered. The user is spared reference to the entire complex matrix. The user's knowledge of characters is limited to those deemed most important by the authoring expert. The key does not accommodate new taxa or modified traits. It is an "end product", not a work in progress.

While dichotomous keys are very useful, random entry examination of taxon-character matrices is a more flexible means of identifying species and more cost-effective means of managing taxonomic information. CATI provides an effective means of implementing random entry keys. Computers eliminate the data management problem. CATI-supported aids such as illustrations reduce the level of expertise required. Reticence on the part of taxonomists to "open their data files" has also recognized by the programmers behind CATI. Programs like INTKEY can produce interactive keys without allowing access to the underlying database.

3. An Overview of Computer Aided Taxonomic Identification (CATI)

The following sections describe CATI in a generic sense. This level of detail is necessary because the future of the system used in this study, DETLA/INTKEY, is uncertain. Development is no longer supported by the Australian government. Open code and commercial versions of this and similar systems are beginning to appear. The following generic description should help any interested manager, ecologist, or systematists to evaluate new software products as they become available.

3.1   Evolution of CATI in Taxonomy

CATI has broad capabilities and can provide an implementation of identification through random entry query of a taxa-character data matrix or provide computer-generated dichotomous keys. The history of CATI is entwined with that of desktop computers and their broad use in taxonomy. Early database programs for use on personal computers were patterned after mainframe applications and became available very early in the development of desktop computers. They combined compact, proprietary formats necessitated by limited memory and slow disk storage, with simple command structure. Data input and query were accomplished through programming employing a limited number of simple commands. Database operation was effectively computer programming. Setting up and maintaining a database require a different expertise than using the database. Users with a particular application in mind, such as taxonomy, were faced with making use of a generic system, or setting up a dedicated system of their own. CATI has taken the route of developing dedicated systems.

The form that CATI's take and the capabilities they possess have been heavily influenced by three interests in taxonomy. The first was facilitation of identification. Taxonomists often employed margin-punched cards (Casey and Perry 1958) as an aid to managing large data sets. Computers afforded a means of managing even larger data sets and extracting results without manual needle sorting. The second was development of more concise ideas about how taxonomic characters (traits) should be coded for computer analysis. This occurred with the advent of numerical taxonomy (Sneath and Sokal 1973). Numerical taxonomy deals with mathematical relationships and requires that characters be concisely defined and consistently recorded. The resulting computer analysis of concise characters directly support the third interest influencing CATI's, cladistic analysis.

Cladistic analysis is based upon the phylogenetic systematics of Hennig (1979), a very formalized methodology and concise terminology used to infer the evolutionary relationship among clades (groups of related taxa). Cladistics has become extremely popular in taxonomy because it reduces subjectivity and allows taxonomic study to bear directly upon questions of evolution (Harvey and Pagel 1991). Cladistics requires the existence of a database of taxa and coded characters. The more comprehensive the analysis, the larger the database must be. Cladistic analyses do not, however, use these databases for identification. Given the appropriate database query subsystem, however, a common taxa-character database can support both cladistics and identification.

3.2 CATI in a Generic Sense

In this study the most widely accepted Computer Aided Taxonomic Identification (CATI) system has been employed, Descriptive Language for Taxonomy (DELTA) (Dallwitz 1980; Dallwitz et al. 1993, 1995, 1999, 2000). CATI is, however, an advancing field, and is best considered in a general manner before one particular version is explained. CATI is a topic that embraces a wide range of activities that apply computer technology to the task of identifying biological specimens. CATI may someday be extraordinarily comprehensive, obtaining images of a subject, recognizing and assessing characters automatically, and identifying the organism by means of comparison with biotic databases maintained by networked CATI systems. Present forms of CATI are much more modest. In effect, they are special database management programs that facilitate the task of comparing the characteristics of an unknown specimen with a database of known species and previously determined characters.

Unfortunately, there is very little literature specifically dedicated to the topic of CATI. Dallwitz (1980) and Pankhurst (1991) remain seminal references. This lack of published information simply reflects that CATI is largely an application of well-known computer technology, and CATI advocates tend to write computer programs rather than publications. CATI such as DELTA are databases with specialized software that inputs data, extracts data by means of query, and deals with formatting issues traditional to taxonomy. Although database theory and application are rapidly advancing, CATI database systems remain simple with only three major components.

Taxa-Characters Database – CATI databases are relational in the sense that they are structured in a way that preserves the relationships among data types. They accommodate different types of data: lists of taxa and lists of the characteristics of those taxa. Such relational databases can be envisioned as a simple table or matrix. Each row of the table contains all entered information about a particular taxa. Each column of the table contains all the information about a particular character. The relationship between taxa and characters is built into the table structure. Complicating matters considerably, the actual data structure in computer memory and storage is rarely the envisioned table. Database systems usually employ proprietary formats intended to provide superior performance with respect to simplicity of data upkeep, speed of query results, compactness, security, scalability, etc. The transition from the envisioned table to the actual database requires use of dedicated software.

Data-Input Subsystem– The method of data entry into a CATI database must accommodate many important tasks: adding, editing, and deleting taxa, adding editing and deleting characteristics, and entering and editing the states of characters for each taxa. If a database actually is a simple table, then such activities could all be carried out with a simple text editor or spreadsheet software. As noted above, however, simple table formats are seldom used, and special input/editing software is usually needed to create and access the proprietary database formats. Such input/editing software may take advantage of graphic user interfaces, or may consist of translator programs that take text files written by simple editors and convert it to the database storage format.

Database Query Subsystem- retrieving useful information from a database requires the ability to ask questions of the database. In the case of CATI, these questions typically take the following form: "list all species names where palps are ventral". The operations are basically that of set theory. The query subsystem may contain many capabilities beyond simple taxon identification. Query subsystems are always dedicated programs, since they must manipulate the proprietary data format, extract results, and present them in a readable format. If the database employs a simple open format (such as a table), then users with programming capabilities could carry out queries with any language implementing functions such as IF, AND, NOT, WHERE, etc. Query systems that support these capabilities are called Structured Query Languages (SQL).

3.3 Selection of DELTA System

At the time this project was undertaken, at least three CATI's were available for use in the desktop computer environment. DELTA (Descriptive Language for Taxonomic Analysis) was the most widely used. PANKEY and CABIKEY were commercially available. The former is an outgrowth of Pankhurst's botany work and is for sale by the Royal Botanical Garden, Edinburgh. CABIKEY is sold by CABI, an international program headquartered in England with a strong emphasis of providing taxonomic capability for economically important taxa (insect pests), especially in developing countries. A few non-commercial programs were also available, but these were generally written for specific applications and were not extensively supported.

DELTA was selected for a variety of reasons:

1. Its use is widely explained in the peer reviewed literature (Aiken et al. 1997; Askevold and O'Brien 1994, Dallwitz 1974, 1980; Dallwitz et al. 1993).

2. Extensive user docmentation is available on-line (Dallwitz et al. 1995, 1999, 2000).

3. It is an exceptionally comprehensive and flexible system

4. It is mature in the sense of having been under development and refinement for over 25 years.

5. It was adopted as an international standard in 1988 by the International Working Group on Taxonomic Databases for Plant Sciences.

As a precautionary note, however, CATI is a developing field, and DELTA has evolved from the time it was first identified as the system of choice for this project. In spite of its current utility, better systems may become available. Most importantly, Australia's CSIRO Entomology concluded support for additional DELTA development after 25 years in 2000. The effect has been to open DELTA up for enhancement by the user community. C+ code replacement for the original compiled FORTRAN programs are now available. Gregor Hagedornof Institute for Plant Virology, Microbiology and Biosafety, at the Federal (Germany) Biological Research Center in Berlin has produced software for translation of DELTA data into the common Microsoft Access database environment. DELTAccess was not used in this project, but is available as freeware at the following web location at the time of writing.

http://www.diversitycampus.net/Workbench/Descriptions/index.html

4. DELTA/INTKEY

4.1 DELTA Versus Generic CATI

DELTA bears some resemblance to the generic CATI system described in chapter 3. The database itself is in a binary format not directly readable by general-use programs. The data input subsytem is in the form of an exceptionally useful DELTA Editor (Dallwitz 1980, Dallwitz et al. 1999). The database query subsystem is not readily identifiable as a single software component. This is the one major drawback to the system. Basic structured query can be accomplished through commands executed by data translation programs, but these are difficult to use. For identification, however, DELTA produces user products such as dichotomous and interactive keys that may be queried by mouse clicks.

4.2 Complexity of Use

DELTA is a flexible format data convention (Dallwitz 1980; Dallwitz et al. 1993, 1995, 1999, 2000) capable of encoding all the types of traits used to identify and classify organisms: counts, measurements, descriptive text, multistate structures, etc. As such, it is a compact means of describing organisms. It is a database about taxa and characters that can be corrected, enlarged, and otherwise modified. A DELTA database can be examined by a variety of specialized computer programs to produce normal text descriptions, traditional keys interactive keys, or modified data suitable for cladistic analysis. INTKEY (Dallwitz 1980; Dallwitz et al. 1993, 1995, 2000) is an especially important companion program that generates interactive keys for identification. DELTA and associated programs are available as compressed download files at

http://Biodiversity.uno.edu/delta

Note: The DELTA system is distributed with restrictions that include license fees and required citation (see Appendix 1). This study was done in full compliance with those restrictions. Users of the polychaete database reported herein must also comply.

DELTA and its associated programs for interactive identification INTKEY are not especially difficult programs to use. The data entry subsystem (DELTA Editor) is now in the form of a multifunction interactive window. For the purposes of this study, the primary database query subsystem is provided by the program INTKEY. It also runs as an interactive window. Successful production of a database and interactive key requires considerable familiarity with a multifunction program CONFOR (Dallwitz 1980; Dallwitz et al.1993). CONFOR combines the functions of a format translator, a structured query language, an error checker, and others. CONFOR may be run from the DELTA editor window, but the user must first create files that provide sequential instructions. Termed directive files, these employ fixed set of commands, a specific format, and a rigid priority sequence. In effect, full use of DELTA and INTKEY require familiarity with programming.

4.3   DELTA/INTKEY Documentation

This section is intended as a very brief introduction to the use of DELTA and the associated programs. It draws heavily from the documentation provided with the software. Rather than a substitute for those documents, the information here is best thought of as a guide to the most effective use of the documents. DELTA offers a range of capabilities to the taxonomist that exceed the purposes of this study. These capabilities are fully described in the cited documents and are not treated here.

Part of the confusion of becoming familiar with DELTA is that it comes with several instruction documents rather than a single comprehensive guide. Unfortunately, the documents do not uniformly reflect the capabilities provided by the latest software revisions. Four documents are required to understand the full DELTA-INTKEY system.

These documents are available as compressed Microsoft Word files at –

http://biodiversity.bio.uno.edu/delta/www/programs.htm

A Primer for the DELTA System Edition 3.01T. R. Partridge, M. J. Dallwitz, and L. Watson April 1999

This 15-page document provides the simplest and most concise description of DELTA. Therefore, it is the best starting place for the new user. Unfortunately, it is out of date with respect to the newer editor's capabilities. The three basic files used by the DELTA system are introduced. The central role of the program CONFOR is explained. CONFOR operates on the DELTA database, creating the other files needed for programs such as INTKEY.

User's Guide to the DELTA Editor Edition 1.03 September 2000 M.J. Dallwitz, T.A. Paine, and E.J. Zurcher

This 24-page document provides instruction on use of the highly versatile editor. The development of a user-friendly data input and editing capability, the DELTA Editor, has greatly facilitated use of the DELTA system. It is possible to create new databases, modify databases, and manipulate all the necessary files and programs with relative ease directly from the editor. The editor employs a Windows graphic users interface with a menu bar making all programs available to the user. Additional manipulation of the created files can be controlled via an "Actions" menu. The editor accepts hand entry of data as well as larger data files. For initial creation of useful databases, this document along with the Primer is an adequate starting place.

User's Guide to the DELTA System: A General System for Processing Taxonomic Descriptions Edition 4.12 M.J. Dallwitz, T.A. Paine, and E.J. Zurcher 2000

This 153-page document bears a 2000 publication date, but does not provide information on the critically important Editor. It is, however, very comprehensive on its treatment of all DELTA component programs. For the critical program CONFOR the many parameters, the complex commands, and formats are explained. The guide is in a technical form common for advanced guides to complex systems.

User's Guide to Intkey: A Program for Interactive Identification and Information Retrieval Edition 1.09 M.J. Dallwitz, T.A. Paine, and E.J. Zurcher 2000

This 24-page document is directed at the end user of INTKEY. INTKEY provides a user-friendly graphic user interface in the Windows environment by which specimens can be identified. The user selects from a list of recorded traits, and enters the state found in the unidentified specimen. After each entry, the list of possible identities is shortened; inapplicable traits are removed. This process repeats until a final identification is reached. The user may enter trait information in a sequence determined by INTKEY to be the most informative (most likely to eliminate possibilities), or in any order preferred. An advanced user can instruct INTKEY to allow for some errors, weight traits, and produce printed descriptions. The documentation is well written, and INTKEY has an adequate help menu.

4.4   An Overview of DELTA and INTKEY Operation

This study developed a total of 12 files and one folder of images. At the core of DELTA is a binary database that can be accessed only by DELTA system programs. In this study, that database is the file **Gulf_Poly.dlt**. The contents of the database can be exchanged (input or output) as three readable files: **Items** (taxa), **Chars** (Characters), and **Specs** (Specifications); in this study, these files are in the folder **Gulf_Poly**. The purpose and contents of each are as follows. Use of illustrations required development of **Images**, a folder of all illustrations, and the files **Timages** and **Cimages**. These files are explained below.

Gulf_Poly.dlt - This is the main database. It is in a binary format and cannot be directly read. It contains all the information of the next five files.

Items - This is an ASCII (simple text) file listing all the taxa in the database along with all the data on the characters for each taxon. The file begins with a line identifying it and then lists each taxon and its characters in a very specific format. The format influences the manner in which other DELTA programs interpret the lines as well as the actual appearance of the name in print or on the computer screen. In this study, the **Items** file contains the names of polychaete families and genera along with their character states. The Items file can be produce by the DELTA Editor by issuing the export command. Alternately, it can be created or edited by a word processor and then imported by the editor. In preparing the polychaete database of this program, both methods were used.

Chars - This is an ASCII file listing all the characters (traits) in the database. The file begins with a line identifying it and then lists each character's name, type, possible values, dependencies on other characters, and control over other characters. The file employs a very specific format that may include embedded printing/display information. The **Chars** file can be produce by the DELTA Editor by issuing the export command. Alternately, it can be created or edited by a word processor and then imported by the editor. In preparing the polychaete database of this program, both methods were used.

Specs - This is also an ASCII file that gives information to the DELTA system on both the nature of the Items and Chars files and how to handle their content. This file gives the user a high level of control over the system, allowing taxa and characters to be used, excluded, or treated in various ways. Unless otherwise instructed, the DELTA editor expects all taxa and characters that have been entered to be used. During this project, the Specs file was used to troubleshoot problems that arose (turning off or on problem characters).

Timages - This file (Taxon Images) is an ASCII file giving a name and path to images illustrating taxa. The illustrations used in this project were scanned from the Ubelacher and Johnson (1984) volumes and converted to 72 pixels/inch jpg files.

Cimages - This file (Character Images) is an ASCII file giving a name and full file path to images illustrating characters. The illustrations used in this study were either scanned from the volumes Ubelacher and Johnson (1984) or created anew by the PI.

Images - This folder contains all the images referred to in the above two files.

Once a database has been successfully created, it can be used to make an interactive key. The program that runs the key is INTKEY. INTKEY does not directly operate on the database, but requires two special files **Iitems** and **Ichars**. These are binary files that are readable only by INTKEY. They are generated by the program CONFOR following instructions found in the directive file **toint**. The compliment of files needed to set up and run INTKEY are as follows.

toint – This is an ASCII file giving CONFOR the commands needed to produce the desired interactive key.

Iitems – This is a binary file written by CONFOR following the instructions in **toint** . It is used by INTKEY to set up taxa-character table.

Ichars – This is a binary file written by CONFOR following the instructions in **toint**. It is used by INTKEY to set up taxa-character table.

Intkey.ink - This is an ASCII file that calls and initialises INTKEY. It points to the name and location of the binary files containing taxa information (Iitems) and character information (Ichars). It also allows for customizing the ordering of the INTKEY display.

Toolbar.inp – This ASCII file controls the toolbar of INTKEY. It activates buttons, points to the bitmap file containing the icon, provides help text, and includes the commands executed when the button is pressed. In this study, custom buttons were developed.

kimages – This small ASCII file points to the jpg file used for startup display.

A summary of the files needed by the end user is as follows:

1. Just use Polychaete interactive key – **Iitems, Ichars, Intkey.ink, Toolbar.inp, kimages,** and the folder **Images.**
2. Examine and alter the polychaete database - **Gulf_Poly.dlt** and the folder **Images.** For simplicity, the readable files **Items, Chars, Specs, Cimages,** and **Timages** may be examined and edited. They can also be extracted from **Gulf_Poly.dlt** using the DELTA Editor.
3. To create an altered interactive key - **Gulf_Poly.dlt,** the folder **Images, toint, Intkey.ink, Toolbar.inp,** and kimages.

4.5   Legal Issues of License and Usage

At the time of writing, the entire DELTA system, programs, and documentation can be downloaded free of charge from http://biodiversity.uno.edu/delta/. This is a comprehensive biodiversity site hosted by the University of New Orleans. Although publicly available, DELTA and its components are neither freeware nor shareware. They are protected by copyright and patent. Use of the software is restricted by the conditions presented in appendix 1. Use of the full system past a trial period of one month requires registration. As per requirements in effect in 2000, a registration fee of $400 was paid during the course of this study. That fee is not transferable to other users.

Users seeking to modify the polychaete database Gulf_poly.dlt must obtain their own copy of the DELTA system and adhere to the restrictions of use. Those merely wanting to use the interactive key must obtain their own copy of INTKEY. That program may be obtained separately from the entire package at the same web site. The conditions of use allow use of INTKEY without registration and without fees.

5. Study Objectives and Methods

5.1 General Statement of Objectives

The present study was undertaken as an initial effort to improve taxonomic QA/QC of benthic marine invertebrates in the Gulf of Mexico. As a result of extensive oil and gas development and increasing multiple use of the Gulf, extensive benthic surveying has taken place and will continue into the future. Incorrect and inconsistent identification seriously threatens the validity of many studies. Adoption of CATI techniques and incorporation of CATI development as a program task seems to be highly advantageous to both the ecological and management community.

The study is atypical of CATI efforts in that the participants are not familiar with the targeted taxa (polychaetes). They are, however, familiar with taxonomy and identification by means of trait examination in a general sense. In the course of this study, they became familiar with CATI as provided by DELTA. In certain regards, this provides a worst-case test of the feasibility of developing interactive keys. Two tasks were proposed.

1. As the primary objective, a database of Gulf of Mexico polychaetes would be developed employing DELTA format and an interactive key created for use with the INTKEY program. The resulting database and key would be distributed to interested users through the biodiversity website maintained at the University of New Orleans (biodiversity.uno.edu). The primary source for the database would be the seven-volume set of Ubelacker and Johnson (1984).

2. As a secondary objective, an evaluation of traditional keys would be made. This task was intended to educate the participants about polychaete anatomy and to provide an understanding of problems in identifying worms.

5.2 Explanation for Limiting the Project to the Polychaetes

The decision to limit the proposed study to the polychaete worms (Annelida: Polychaeta) was based upon recognition of four factors. First, evaluation of CATI methods to management needed to be done on a restricted fauna group. Second, the contribution of polychaetes to overall biodiversity is so great that consideration of that taxon would provide maximum benefit from the initial effort. Third, from our own experience we felt that correct sorting and identification of polychaetes may be the most error prone aspect of benthic analysis and most in need of improvement. Forth, there is already an initial DELTA database for polychaetes being compiled and there is a substantial body of expertise to draw from in terms of people, publications, and collections.

The primary literature for the Gulf of Mexico polychaetes is the MMS-sponsored taxonomic series produced by Vittor and Associates (Uebelacker and Johnson 1984). This series treats 593 species of polychaetes in 288 genera, and 59 families. Forty-one percent of these species were new to science. Supplementing Vittor's work is the doctoral dissertation of Hubbard (1997). Dr. Hubbard worked with the slope-depth polychaetes collected during a study funded by MMS, the Northern Gulf of Mexico Continental Slope Study (Gallaway 1989) discusses 446 species of the 635 nominal species reported in that study.

The two principal references used to develop the interactive key are quite different in purpose and content. Uebelacker and Johnson (1984) is in the style of a traditional monograph providing both brief diagnoses of taxa, more detailed descriptions, illustrations, a glossary of terms, and discussion as to the taxonomic value of the traits. As such it is a rich source of information. Hubbard (1997) is primarily an ecological study. The important taxonomic information is provided in an appendix and is limited to very brief diagnoses without illustration or glossary. Therefore, taxa not also treated by Uebelacker and Johnson (1984) may have relatively little character information coded about them.

By far the most difficult task in creating a DELTA database is determining which characters are to be included. In this study that decision was limited by the information in the primary references. In an ideal situation, however, the database would be developed with ready access to specimens and an overall appreciation of polychaete anatomy. Fortunately, some order is beginning to emerge from the chaos of polychaete systematics and anatomy. Rouse and Fauchald (1995, 1997), Fauchald and Rouse (1997), and Rouse and Pleijel (2001) provided considerable help in delineating characters.

While this study has been a stand-alone program, it has benefited from other efforts. The Natural History Museum in London has posted a simple random entry key to 50 major families of polychaetes that makes use of only 26 traits with fewer than five states,

http://www.nhm.ac.uk/zoology/taxinf/index2.html

The Victoria Museum in Australia is carrying out a long-term project that has produced keys to five families at this time. No key to families is presented, but descriptions of selected families are given.

http://www.museum.vic.gov.au/poly/families.html

6. Assessing Difficulties in Traditional Polychaete Keys

6.1 Concept of Dichotomous Keys

Dichotomous keys are the most common traditional means of identifying organisms. MMS has made a considerable contribution to the quality assurance of invertebrate identification through support of the Ubelacker and Johnson (1984) polychaete keys and the numerous keys included in the Taxonomic Atlas of the Benthic Fauna of the Santa Maria Basin and Western Santa Barbara Channel (Blake and Hilbig 1994). This present study examines the feasibility of replacing traditional keys with trait databases and interactive keys.

Ideally, a key represents the thoughtful distillation of all that is known about morphological variation of a particular group of organisms. The writer of keys attempts to identify and order a subset of all that is known. This subset and its order should allow correct and consistent identification with a minimal number of traits being used. There are two primary benefits of dichotomous keys. First, that they require the user to be familiar with only a relatively small set of anatomical terms. Second, they provide a reference by which the quality of identifications can be partially judged. Unfortunately there are at least three major drawbacks with keys. First, the user is forced to follow an inflexible sequence of questions. Damage to a few key traits may effectively render a key useless. Second, although providing a QA reference, the actual assurance gained by a key is hard to access. Third, upgrading of a key can be a difficult undertaking.

There appear to be no accepted standards for assessing the utility of keys. It is, however, easy to identify desirable properties. Ideally, the taxa being identified fit cleanly into larger groups; the traits that determine group membership have absolute group fidelity. These larger groups also fit cleanly into even larger groups as determined by other high-fidelity traits. In the entire hierarchy of the taxa, there is never any ambiguity as into which group a taxon should be placed. The traits that determine membership in a group should be simple, rather than compound. This allows the questions in the key to be very simple. The structure of keys may be judged by these standards:

1. Key size – The total number of questions in a key will depend on the number of taxa and the efficiency with which the questions discriminate among them. The theoretical minimal number of questions is given by

   $Q_{min} = N-1$ where N = number of taxa.

2. Question sequence length – The number of questions that must be correctly answered to arrive at a final identification is also dependent on the number of taxa and the efficiency with which the questions discriminate among them. A minimum average sequence length is given by

   $S_L = \log_2(N)$.

3. Complexity of Questions – Simple questions are based upon a single character. As the number of characters included in a question increase, the complexity goes up. Complexity may be evaluated by counting characters.

4. Ambiguity of Questions – Questions which can be answered with certainty and without subjectivity are unambiguous. Terms such as sometimes, often, and some what increase ambiguity. Ill-defined descriptive terms that require subjective user judgement also increase ambiguity. Ambiguity can be evaluated by counting conditional terms.

6.2　Trial Evaluation Using the Blake Key to Polychaete Families

Preparatory to developing a DELTA/INTKEY interactive key to the polychaetes a careful examination of existing traditional keys was undertaken for three purposes. First, providing the instruction needed to assist students provided the PI with a strong introduction to polychaete anatomy. Second, it helped identify traits that might be especially troublesome in identification. Third, it was a trial attempt to provide quality assurance review of a key produced for management purpose.

Blake's (1994) key to polychaete families was selected for use. Alternatives were the keys contained in Ubelacker and Johnson (1984) and Fauchald (1977). Unfortunately, the former lacks an initial key to families. Fauchald's key to the families and genera of polychaetes was a seminal book in many regards. It attempted to bring some order to the polychaetes at the superfamily level. It streamlined the terminology of polychaete morphology, and it provided ecologists with a vital tool for the identification of worms. It was, however, rendered somewhat out of date by the superfamily scheme proposed by Pettibone (1982). Blake (1994) incorporated Pettibone's hierarchy in a regional key for polychaetes of southern California. While regional in scope, Blake's key includes 58 family-level taxa. These include 56 common families and two based upon splitting of the families Oweniidae and Amperetidae. The key resolves the taxa with a total of 60 dichotomies aided by a glossary of approximately 250 descriptive terms (Figure 6-1).

With respect to the general criteria presented in section 3.1, Blake has produced a well-structured key. It resolves 58 family-level taxa with only 60 questions, only 2 more than the theoretical minimal number, Q_{min}. The average number of questions that must be answered to arrive at a final identification is 9.7, not too much higher than the ideal of six. The length of question series ranged from 1 to 14. The questions tend to be somewhat complex, containing an average of 3.5 traits with a range of one to six per question. Thirty eight percent of the questions are made somewhat ambiguous by the use of conditional and subjective terms.

The methodology of evaluation was simple. Ten undergraduate students were recruited from the students enrolled in the oceanography survey course in oceanography. The students were given the glossary of terms provided by Blake and Hilbig (1994) and instructed to study them. Students met separately with the PI and were given twenty-five polychaetes (Table 6.1) to identify using a stereo microscope. Polychaetes were selected for which specimens were readily available. To prevent destruction of the specimen, illustrations of setae were provided when needed. Students proceeded through the key with minimal prompting. On each species, identification proceeded until a wrong answer was given. "Backing up" in the key to retry a question was not allowed. The sequence of species was the same for all trials.

Table 6.1. Polychaetes used and results from trial evaluation using Blake's key to families.

FAMILY	Genus	Species	Correct out of 10
Capitellidae	*Mediomastus*	*californiensis*	4
Chrysopetalidae	*Paleanotus*	*heteroseta*	7
Cirratulidae	*Tharyx*	*cf. annulosus*	0
Dorvilleidae	*Protodorvillea*	*kefersteini*	0
Eunicidae	*Eunice*	*vittata*	3
Glyceridae	*Glycera*	*papillosa*	2
Goniadidae	*Goniadides*	*carolinae*	4
Lumbrineridae	*Lumbrineris*	*tenuis*	4
Magelonidae	*Magelona*	*pettiboneae*	6
Maldanidae	*Asychis*	*elongatus*	4
Nephtyidae	*Aglaophamus*	*verrilli*	2
Nephtyidae	*Nephtys*	*incisa*	4
Nereidae	*Ceratocephale*	*oculata*	2
Nereidae	*Nereis*	*riisei*	2
Onuphidae	*Diopatra*	*cuprea*	1
Opheliidae	*Armandia*	*maculata*	2
Oweniidae	*Myriochele*	*oculata*	1
Pilargidae	*Sigambra*	*tentaculata*	3
Poecilochaetidae	*Poecilochaetus*	*johnsoni*	1
Sabellidae	*Euchone*	*incolor*	0
Spionidae	*Laonice*	*cirrata*	2
Spionidae	*Paraprionospio*	*pinnata*	2
Syllidae	*Exogone*	*dispar*	4
Syllidae	*Haplosyllis*	*spongicola*	4
Trichobranchidae	*Terebellides*	*stroemi*	1

The title "Blake Key to Families Trial Results" appears at the top of the table.

The trials did not provide as clear guidance on difficult traits. Indeed, traits per se were not difficult to assess. The key, however, employed many questions that were complex in the sense of dealing with up to six traits. Out of 250 separate attempts at identification to family; 65 were successful. Considering that the users were naive and "backing up" forbidden, this was quite good. Success on the key questions 1, 2, 8, 27, 29, 30, 41 was exceptionally good. These questions focused upon body shape, elytra, pharynx, chitin shield, retractile buccal tentacles, buccal segment, and setal hooks. All were relatively simple and could be determined without dissection. Only two dealt with setae, and these did not address details of structure or fine points of distribution. Questions that were commonly missed often asked fine points about setal distribution and were generally more complex in the sense of containing multiple parts.

The process of "keying out" polychaetes and the results of the student trial can be shown as a tree (Figure 6.1). Of all the families included in the key, bold lines lead to the examples given in the trials. The numbers of each node (branch point question) refer to the actual question numbers in Blake's key. Shaded nodes represent the commonly missed questions. Students did a good job of answering questions that sorted the taxa into five main divisions. Finer resolution, however, required technically complex examination of parapodia and chaetae. Even with the aid of illustrations, these questions were missed by the unexperienced user. A similar problem can be expected with interactive keys.

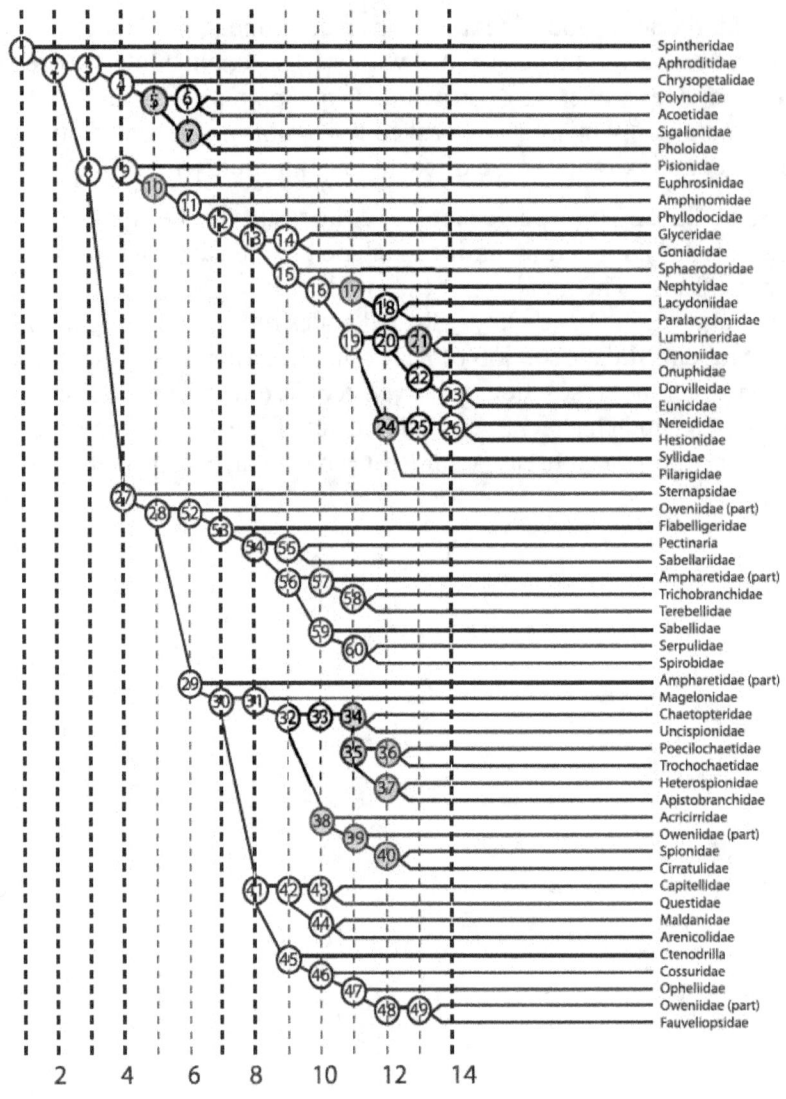

Spintheridae
Aphroditidae
Chrysopetalidae
Polynoidae
Acoetidae
Sigalionidae
Pholoidae
Pisionidae
Euphrosinidae
Amphinomidae
Phyllodocidae
Glyceridae
Goniadidae
Sphaerodoridae
Nephtyidae
Lacydoniidae
Paralacydoniidae
Lumbrineridae
Oenoniidae
Onuphidae
Dorvilleidae
Eunicidae
Nereididae
Hesionidae
Syllidae
Pilargidae
Sternapsidae
Oweniidae (part)
Flabelligeridae
Pectinaria
Sabellariidae
Ampharetidae (part)
Trichobranchidae
Terebellidae
Sabellidae
Serpulidae
Spirobidae
Ampharetidae (part)
Magelonidae
Chaetopteridae
Uncispionidae
Poecilochaetidae
Trochochaetidae
Heterospionidae
Apistobranchidae
Acricirridae
Oweniidae (part)
Spionidae
Cirratulidae
Capitellidae
Questidae
Maldanidae
Arenicolidae
Ctenodrilla
Cossuridae
Opheliidae
Oweniidae (part)
Fauveliopsidae

2   4   6   8   10   12   14

Answer Sequence Length to Final Identification

Figure 6-1 Blake's key to families graphed to show size and sequence lengths.
Shaded questions were most often missed.

7. Development of the Gulf_Poly Database and Interactive Key

7.1 Selection of Taxa

A master list was developed of all families, genera, and species reported in five MMS-supported benthic surveys based on the synthesis of Carney (1993): STBS (South Texas Baseline Study), CGP (Central Gulf Platform), MAFLA (Mississippi. Alabama, Florida), SWFL (Southwest Florida), and NGMCS (Northern Gulf of Mexico Continental Slope Study). These lists were then compared to the taxa treated in Ubelacker and Johnson (1984) and Hubbard (1997). It should be noted that there is no readily available, high quality, database of the fauna collected during Gulf of Mexico surveying and monitoring. Each MMS-supported study has submitted faunal data to the National Oceanographic Data Center. The quality of those archives varies greatly, and they are not actively maintained, corrected, etc.

7.2 Selection of Characters

The original intent of this study was to translate the data contained in the Vittor text into a DELTA format database with minimal modification. Listing all the characters found in genus and species description began this task. The impracticality of this approach was quickly obvious when the number of characters exceeded 250 with only 80 species covered. This multitude of traits was only in part due to the morphological diversity of polychaetes. A great deal was due to a subjective terminology applied inconsistently across families. This was especially the case for descriptions of parapodia structures.

It was deemed necessary to reduce jargon while not straying far from the original text. Initially, six working character groups were established upon published family descriptions. These were head, anterior segments, branchi, parapodia, and setae. Starting with the head working group, structures found on all Vittor genera and species were compiled. Thus, antennae, palps, eyes, and pharynx were added as characters with many different states. When the number of states became confusing or unsuitable, the character would be split into multiple characters. Unfortunately, this progressing to finer and finer levels of character resolution resulted in some difficulties. First, it made the database quite complex. Second, it resulted in many characters that had to be left uncoded due to inconsistent treatment in the Ubelacker and Johnson (1984) or the brevity of Hubbard (1997). A subsequent attempt to simplify the characters was to create summary characters such as head-complex versus head-simple. These allow a user to progress through an interactive key without having to provide a great deal of detail but did not faithfully preserve the complexity of the fauna.

Development of the entire database proceeded very similarly to the above example for head-related structures. Each major trait group was taken one at a time. All generic and species variation was catalogued and then an effort made to simplify the complexity. The last trait group treated was the setae. After all characters were established, the illustrations in Vittor were examined to determine the feasibility of illustrating the character states. This resulted in some restructuring of the characters.

7.3   Character Problem Areas

Since DELTA databases are always open for revision, it is important to identify components in which future work is needed. These all require additional study of polychaete specimens and are beyond the scope and expertise of the present project. Three areas that require attention are:

1. Antennae, tentacles, and palps – there needs to be consistent application of these terms based upon homology and analogy. Length should be treated in a consistent manner relative to other body dimensions. Shape, thickness, and ornamentation should be similarly standardized. Unfortunately, the database produced here perpetuates inconsistent usages.

2. Branchi - there needs to be consistent application of this term based upon homology and analogy. Length should be treated in a consistent manner relative to other body dimensions. Shape, thickness, and ornamentation should be similarly standardized. A better means of reporting position of branchi on and off the parapodia needs to be developed.

3. Parapodia – there needs to be consistent application of terms based upon homology and analogy. Length should be treated in a consistent manner relative to other body dimensions. Shape, thickness, and ornamentation should be similarly standardized. Even very basic terms such as uniramous, sub-biramous, and biramous seem to be applied inconsistently due to anterior-posterior complexities. Terms such as "cirrus" are confusingly used to refer both to a structure and a shape. Thus, many "cirri" and not the least "cirriform".

8. Instructions for Use of Gulf Polychaete Interactive Key

This chapter is intended as a general-purpose guide to downloading, installing, and running the DELTA system, including INTKEY. More detailed information may be found in the downloaded documents.

8.1 Downloading and Installing the DELTA SYSTEM

At the time of writing, the DELTA system may be downloaded from

http://www.biodiversity.uno.edu/delta/

- *Once that web page is displayed, select –*

- *Programs and documentation. Then select*

- *All programs (including Intkey).*

A 5.71 Mbytes self-extracting file, delt32.exe, will be downloaded to your computer and placed in the directory structure as indicated in a task window. Clicking on the icon will run an installation wizard prompting the user through installation. When installed, the DELTA system contains a confusing array of files. Some are programs (Triangle icon); others are example, data, and example digital databases. Documentation is contained as a series of MS WORD files in the **doc** folder.

8.2 Downloading and Unzipping the Gulf Polychaete Database

The necessary files may be downloaded from:

http://www.biodiversity.uno.edu/delta/www/data.htm

Once that web page has opened, click on - Polychaetes - Gulf of Mexico

A zip compressed archive will be downloaded to a location on the computer as directed by the user. The archive must be uncompressed by software obtained by the users following all relevant license restrictions. The decompressed folder contains the following files:

Chars - ASCII file of characters used

Items - ASCII file of taxa

Gulf_poly.dlt – Binary database readable by the DELTA system programs

Iimages – Images used to illustrate taxa in JPEG format.

Timages – Images used to illustrate taxa in JPEG format.

8.3 Running INTKEY

The program may be run by double clicking on the file /Gulf_Polychaetes/ intkey.ink. If defaults were used when installing DELTA and INTKEY, the operating system will locate intkey5.exe and run it. If prompted to find intkey5.exe, double click on its icon and then use its browser to locate /Gulf_Polychaetes/. Once running the program will display a startup tiles and figure. Clicking on it brings up the working window (Figure 8-1).

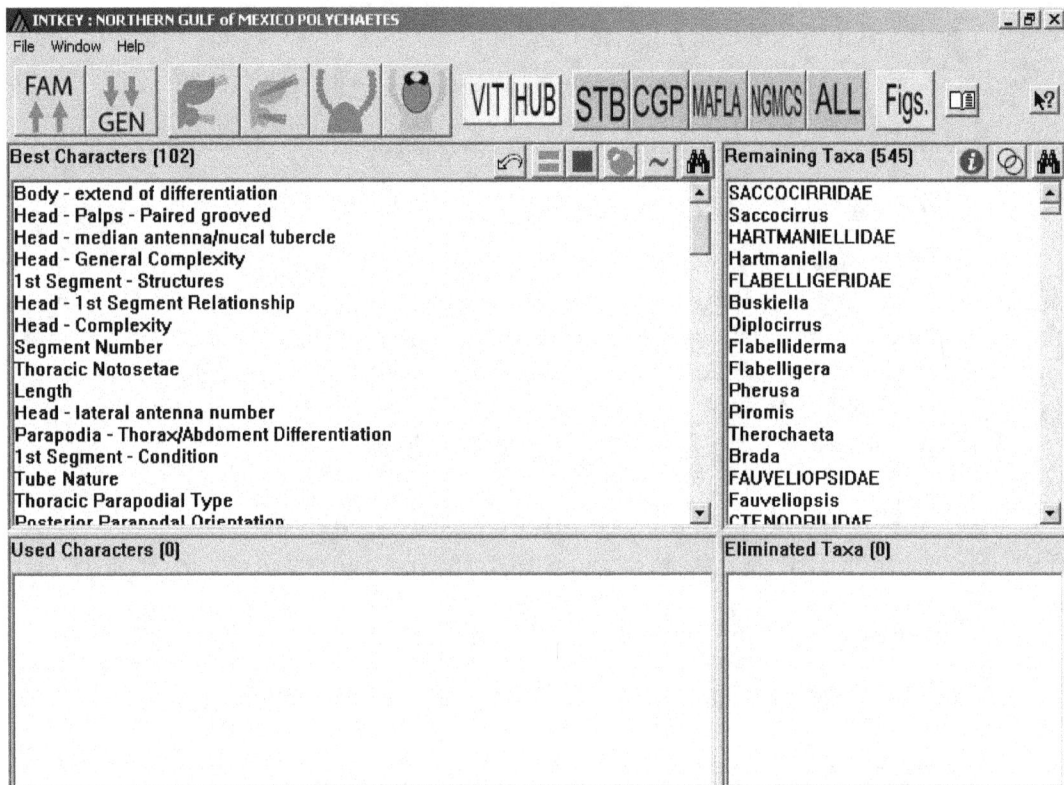

Figure 8-1 INTKEY working window shows taxa and characters.

Use of the working window is very well explained in the INTKEY documentation, and will not be repeated here. Additional functionality has, however, been added in the form of action buttons.

Taxonomic Level Functionality

The ability to identify organisms to different taxonomic levels (species, genus, subfamily, family, etc.) is a highly desirable feature of any key. In the case of Uebelacker and Johnson (1984), identification to family is necessary to make use of the family-level chapters. Unfortunately, INTKEY does not at this time support hierarchical summation in which the traits for species can be summed into genera, families, etc. An attempt has been made to provide such functionality by including both families and genera in the database. Families are always in boldface capital letters and precede their genera in the taxa list.

 **FAMily** button limits taxa set to families.

 **GENus** button limits taxa to genera.

Principal Reference Functionality

 HUBbard button limits taxa set to those treated in Hubbard (1997). These are the deep-water taxa.

 VITtor button limits taxa set to those treated in Ubelacker and Johnson (1984). These are the continental shelf taxa.

Study and Zoogeographic Functionality

The Delta database and the INTKEY interactive key that it supports are not intended as a geographic information system (GIS). At the family and genus level of the interactive key, geographic position is a weak trait. The same is true for depth. Many genera are eurybathal, and depth of collection does not narrow down the possible taxa that an unknown animal may be. Nevertheless, the interactive key incorporates the ability to limit the taxa set to a particular geographically restricted study. With the exception of the Northern Gulf of Mexico Continental Slope study (Gallaway 1989, Hubbard 1997), the geography of sampling is well described in Ubelacker and Johnson (1984).

 STB button limits taxa set to those species collected by the South Texas Baseline Study. Ubelacker and Johnson (1984) intermingle this data with that obtained from the geographically overlapping IXTOC study.

 CGP button limits taxa set to those species collected by the Central Gulf Platform Study.

 MAFLA button limits taxa set to those species collected by the Mississippi, Alabama, and Florida Study. Samples were taken along the coasts of the respective states.

 SWFL button limits taxa set to those species collected by the Southwest Florida Study. Samples were taken along the west coast of Florida.

NGMCS button limits taxa set to those genera collected by the Northern Gulf of Mexico Continental Slope study (Galloway 1988) beyond the edge of the continental shelf. Functionally, the action of the button is identical to the HUB button.

 ALL button includes all studies.

Character Set Selection Functionality

The characters coded in this study may be intimidating to the novice user, and many may not be applicable when damaged specimens are encountered. This will especially be the case when detailed examination of setae under high magnification is required. In such instances a partial identification may suffice, followed by examination of illustrations. The ability to restrict the trait set has been included with action buttons.

 HEAD button limits traits to those associated with the head and the first 2 segments past the head.

 PHARYNX button limits traits to those associated with the everted pharynx and its structures. Many taxa lack such a pharynx, but it is a dramatic feature when present.

 PARAPODIA button limits traits to those associated with the parapodia after the head and first two segments. These can be difficult traits to use since they depend upon use of a subjective nomenclature to describe shapes.

 Setae (Chaetae) button limits traits to those associated with the setae. Effective use of these traits requires magnification of at least 100X.

Final Action

It is to be expected that use of the interactive key will not always narrow the search to a single genus. Once the search has produced a short list of candidate taxa, many users will prefer to look at the illustrations before making a final decision. All the illustrations in Ubelacker and Johnson (1984) have been included in the interactive key. They may be viewed by means of an action button.

Figs. Brings up a dialog box that lets the user select the figures to be examined on screen.

9. Unresolved Issues and Recommendations

9.1 Considering Issues and Recommendations

This exercise in database and interactive key development has shown that it is feasible to take fairly comprehensive taxonomic guides and convert them into a computer-accessed format. This is, however, just a first step. Many more steps could be taken. The polychaete database needs revision and improvement; other important taxa need consideration as well. MMS has demonstrated its commitment to taxonomic quality assurance through the production of Ubelacker and Johnson (1984), Blake (1994), this report, and continued support for the voucher collections at the US National Museum of Natural History. Systematic Focus

Surveys and monitoring typically collect meiofauna, macrofauna, and megafauna. Internationally, the macrofauna have been the major source of diversity and population density data. The same is true for the Gulf of Mexico and argues for a focus upon polychaetes, pericarid crustaceans, and mollusc. This study has begun the polychaete work, and an international effort to develop DELTA databases for crustaceans is underway (www.crustacea.net) (Lowry 1999 onwards, Lowry and Springthorpe 2001, Ahyong and Lowry 2001).

9.2 Taxonomic Resolution

A major disappointment of this project was that a species-level interactive key proved impractical without participation by a team of collaborators expert in the various polychaete families considered. Without such assistance in identifying homologous and analogous characters, it would have been necessary to create as many as 500 characters. The resulting interactive key would have been too complex to serve a useful purpose. From trial testing of the interactive key, it is very effective at identifying to family using different combinations of characters. Performance at the genus level is less reliable. As a practical matter, the key provides ready access to all the illustrations of Ubelacker and Johnson (1984). These may prove helpful in a final identification once the key has limited possibilities.

Given the tremendous diversity of polychaetes in the Gulf of Mexico and elsewhere, do survey and monitoring studies really need species-level identification? Should management agencies like MMS contribute to the development DELTA databases that support species-level ID? Unfortunately, no simple answer is possible without considerable more study. Arguing for species-level identification are two very important points.

1. Ecological theory is based upon the premise that the major interactions between organisms and the environment can be effectively understood and predicted at the species or population level. All organisms within a species or population are envisioned as playing similar roles. If the faunal variability found in survey and monitoring is ever to be understood and predicted (not the case now), then a strong link to ecological theory at the species level will be required.

2. Most MMS-supported surveying and monitoring up to this time have required species-level identification for at least some faunal components. This history has the effect of establishing that taxonomic as the de facto standard. Identification only at higher levels may lead to the charge that studies are ill designed and ineffective.

Arguing against the need for species-level identification are two equally valid points.

1. Given the declining pool of trained taxonomic experts, identification to species may be effectively impossible for some taxa. This is especially the case for the deep sea or other pioneer areas containing many undescribed species. It may be better to get correct and consistent identification to genus than erroneous and inconsistent identification to species.

2. Assessment of faunal change and impact may not require total faunal inventory at the species level (Ferraro and Cole 1990). Higher taxa might suffice or functional groups such as feeding guilds (Fauchald and Jumar 1979). As attractive as this argument is to management, it has not been sufficiently studied to be adopted as a matter of policy.

9.3   Implementation

Agencies which currently pay for taxonomic expertise can begin developing CATI databases with minimal change in policy and funding level. MMS studies carry the requirement that faunal data be archived and voucher specimens maintained. An added requirement would be that a taxonomic database for all species encountered also be submitted. These databases would be provided by the consulting taxonomists with modest increased costs. When comprehensive treatments are needed, such as Ubelacker and Johnson (1984) or Blake (1994), those project-generated databases could be organized, edited, improved as needed and issued.

9.4   Recommendations

The purpose of this study was to see if CATI held potential for improvement of identifications in any activity of MMS that required faunal surveying. While the polychaete database produced requires trial-and-error evaluation and additional refinement, it is a first step highly amenable to development and improvement. It also provides easy access to much of the data and all the illustrations in Ubelacker and Johnson. As such, it is an adequate proof of method. Additional development of CATI for MMS purposes should be directed towards MMS' mission needs. These can be identified by region and by contribution to overall benthic population or benthic diversity. The fauna of the Gulf of Mexico should have highest priority. Within that region, polychaetes, pericarid crustacea, and molluscs should be given the highest priority. The following general recommendations should be considered.

1. Traditional key production should no longer be undertaken and should be replaced by the more versatile production of CATI databases.

2. The DELTA system is presently the CATI application of choice. Improvement of future CATI systems should be encouraged and taxonomic

data management understood in the context of larger data management strategies.

3. The practice of supporting multiple experts as used for Ubelacker and Johnson (1984) and Blake (1994) should be continued. Where the required experts lack familiarity with DELTA, training and collaboration with CATI experts should be included in task orders.

4. All development of databases must be preceded by a separate scoping phase where the adequacy of the existing published accounts is evaluated, the availability of specimens determined, and the required effort and mix of expertise assessed.

5. When a MMS contractor provides taxonomic expertise, descriptions of all new taxa encountered should be provided in DELTA format for incorporation into developing databases in a timely manner.

10. Literature Cited

Ahyong, S.T. and J.K. Lowry. 2001 onwards. Stomatopoda: Families. Version 1. http://www.crustacea.net.

Aiken, S. G., M. J. Dallwitz, C. L.McJannet, and L. L. Consaul. 1997. Biodiversity among Festuca (Poaceae) in North America: Diagnostic evidence from DELTA and clustering programs, and an INTKEY package for interactive, illustrated identification and information retrieval. Canadian Journal of Botany 75: 1,527–1,555.

Askevold, I. S. and C. W. O'Brien. 1994. DELTA, an invaluable computer program for generation of taxonomic monographs. Annals Entomological Society America 87: 1–16.

Blake J.A. and B. Hilberg (eds). 1994. Taxonomic atlas of the benthic fauna of the Santa Maria Basin and Western Santa Barbara. U.S. Dept. of the Interior, Minerals Management Service, Pacific OCS Region, Camarillo, CA. OCS Study MMS 93-0030. 14 vols.

Blake, J.A. 1994. Introduction to the polychaeta. In: Blake, J.A. and B. Hilberg (eds). Taxonomic atlas of the benthic fauna of the Santa Maria Basin and Western Santa Barbara Channel: The annelida Part 1 Oligichaeta and polychaeta: Phyllodocida (Phyllodocidae to Paralacydonidae). U.S. Dept. of the Interior, Minerals Management Service, Pacific OCS Region, Camarillo, CA. OCS Study MMS 93-0030. Vol. 4. Pp. 39-101.

Carney, R.S. 1987. A review of study designs for the detection of long-term environmental effects of offshore petroleum activities. In: Boesch, D. and N. Rabalais (eds). Long-term environmental effects of offshore oil and gas development. London: Elsevier Applied Science. Pp. 652-690.

Carney, R.S. 1993. Review and reexamination of OCS spatial-temporal variability as determined by MMS studies in the Gulf of Mexico. U.S. Dept. of the Interior Minerals Managment Sertvice, New Orleans La. OCS Study MMS 93-0041. 210 pp.

Carney, R.S. 1996. On the adequacy and improvement of marine benthos pre-impact surveys: examples from the Gulf of Mexico outer continental shelf. In Schmitt, R.J. and C.W. Osenberg (eds.). Dectecting ecological impact: Concepts and applications in coastal habitats. New York: Academic Press. Pp. 295-313.

Casey, R.S. and J.W. Perry (eds.). 1958. Punched cards: Their applications to science and industry, 2nd ed. New York: Reinhold Publishing Corp. 697 pp.

Dallwitz, M. J. 1974. A flexible computer program for generating identification keys. Systematic Zoology 23:7-50.

Dallwitz, M. J., T. A. Paine, and E. J. Zurcher. 1993. User's guide to the DELTA System: a general system for processing taxonomic descriptions: quality control of biological surveys. Marine Pollution Bulletin 19:506–512.

Dallwitz, M. J., T. A. Paine, and E. J. Zurcher. 1995. User's guide to INTKEY: a program for interactive identification and information retrieval, 1st edition. http://biodiversity.uno.edu/delta/

Dallwitz, M. J., T. A. Paine, and E. J. Zurcher. 1999. User's guide to the DELTA editor. http://biodiversity.uno.edu/delta/

Dallwitz, M. J., T. A. Paine, and E. J. Zurcher. 2000. Principles of interactive keys. http://biodiversity.uno.edu/delta/

Dallwitz, M. J.1993. DELTA and INTKEY. In: Fortuner, R. (ed.). Advances in computer methods for systematic biology: Artificial intelligence, databases, computer vision. Baltimore, MD: The Johns Hopkins University Press. Pp. 287–296.

Dallwitz, M.J. 1980. A general system for coding taxonomic descriptions. Taxon 29:6–41.

Fauchald, K. 1977. The polychaete worms. Definitions and keys to the genera and families. Natural History Museum of Los Angeles County Science Series 28:1-188.

Fauchald, K. and G.W. Rouse. 1997. Polychaete systematics: Past and present. Zoologica Scripta 26:71-138.

Fauchald, K. and P.A. Jumars. 1979. The diet of worms: An analysis of polychaete feeding guilds. Oceanography and Marine Biology 17:193-284.

Ferraro,S.P. and F.A. Cole, 1990. Taxonomic level and sample size sufficient for assessing pollution impacts on the southern California bight macrobenthos. Marine Ecology Progress Series 67:251-262.

Gallaway, B.J. (ed.). 1989. Northern Gulf of Mexico Continental Slope Study: Annual Report, Year 4. Vols. I-III Appendices. Annual report submitted to the Minerals Management Service, New Orleans, La. OCS Study MMS 87-0060.

Harvey, P.H. and M. D. Pagel. 1991. The comparative method in evolutionary biology. Oxford & New York: Oxford University Press. 239 pp.

Hennig, W. 1979. Phylogenetic systematics. Translated by D.D. Davis and R. Zangerl. Urbana, IL: University of Illinois Press. 263 pp.

Hubbard, F. 1997. Polychaete fauna of the northern Gulf of Mexico continental slope. PhD Dissertation, Texas A&M University.

Lowry, J.K. 1999 onwards. Crustacea, the higher taxa: descriptions, illustrations, identification, and information retrieval. Version: 2. http://www.crustacea.net/

Lowry, J.K. and R.T. Springthorpe. 2001 onwards. Amphipoda: families. Version 1: 2. http://www.crustacea.net/

Lowry, J.K. and R.T. Springthorpe. 2000 onwards. Australian amphipoda: Ampeliscidae descriptions, illustrations, identification and retrieval. http://www.crustacea.net.

Mayr, E. and P.D. Ashlock. 1991. Principles of systematic zoology, 2nd edition. New York: McGraw-Hill. 475 pp.

Pankhurst, R.J. 1991. Practical taxonomic computing. Cambridge & New York: Cambridge University Press. 202 pp.

Pettibone, M.H. 1982. Annelida. In: Parker, S.P. (ed.). Synopsis and classification of living organisms. New York: McGraw-Hill. Pp. 1-43.

Rouse, G.W. and K. Fauchald. 1995. The articulation of annelids. Zoologica Scripta 24: 269-301.

Rouse, G.W. and K. Fauchald. 1997. Cladistics and polychaetes. Zoologica Scripta 26: 139-204.

Rouse, G.W. and F. Pleijel. 2001. Polychaetes. Cambridge: Oxford University Press. 354 pp.

Sneath, P.H.A. and R.R. Sokal. 1973. Numerical taxonomy: The principles and practise of numerical classification. San Francisco, CA: W.H. Freeman and Company. 573 pp.

Scott, P. and J.A. Blake. 1997. Taxonomic atlas of the benthic fauna of the Santa Maria Basin and Western Santa Barbara basins. Santa Barbara, CA: Santa Barbara Museum Natural History. 14 vols.

Uebelacker, J.M. and P.G. Johnson. 1984. Taxonomic guide to the polychaetes of the northern Gulf of Mexico. Final report to the U.S. Dept. of the Interior, Minerals Management Service. 7 vols.

Appendix 1. Conditions of Use and Software Registration Form

THE DELTA SYSTEM - CONDITIONS OF USE

14 September 2000

M. J. Dallwitz, T. A. Paine, and E. J. Zurcher

CSIRO Entomology, GPO Box 1700

Canberra ACT 2601, Australia

Phone +61 2 6246 4075 Fax +61 2 6246 4000

Email delta@ento.csiro.au

INTRODUCTION

The DELTA format (DEscription Language for TAxonomy) is a flexible method for encoding taxonomic descriptions for computer processing. DELTA-format data can be used to produce natural-language descriptions, conventional and interactive keys, and cladistic and phenetic classifications.

The DELTA System supplied by CSIRO Entomology comprises: Intkey, a program for interactive identification and information retrieval; the DELTA Editor, a program for creating and editing DELTA data; Confor, a program for translating DELTA data into other formats; various other programs; documentation, including User's Guide to the DELTA Editor and User's Guide to the DELTA System; and sample data files.

OBTAINING THE PROGRAMS

The DELTA System and various data sets are available from the DELTA Home

Page at http://biodiversity.uno.edu/delta/

CONDITIONS OF USE

Registration   Use of any of the programs except Intkey beyond a test period of one month is prohibited unless you have registered, or are a student at an organization where the programs have been registered. Intkey may be used without registration, subject to the other conditions in this document.

Citation   If use of the programs contributes to a publication, you must include appropriate citations (see User's Guide to the DELTA System), and send a copy of the publication to the DELTA authors.

Use or distribution for financial gain Use or distribution of the programs for financial gain is prohibited unless you have entered into a License Agreement for such use or distribution.

Redistribution   You may distribute the programs provided you do not receive a financial gain from such distribution, and you include the files Use.txt (this document) and Register.txt (registration and order form).

Support	Registered users are entitled to free support for clarification of the programs or documentation. Reported program bugs will be fixed promptly.Significant help with the design, analysis, or presentation of data should be treated as collaboration, and lead to joint publications.
	There is a mailing list, DELTA-L, for discussion of DELTA and announcements of updates - see the Installation Guide for details. Requests for support should be sent to delta@ento.csiro.au, or to DELTA-L.
Liability	Terms, conditions, warranties, or representations, relating in any way to the programs, are excluded, except where expressly provided to the contrary in these conditions of use. CSIRO or its employees shall not be liable for any loss, damage, or injury (including without limitation any loss of profit, indirect, consequential, or incidental loss, damage, or injury) arising from the use of the programs.

REGISTRATION FEES AND EXEMPTIONS

A registration and order form is provided in the file Register.txt. The fees are subject to chang without notice.

Multi-user registration	The fee for registering several users within the same organization is based on the number of people who could be using the programs simultaneously, excluding users who are exempt from the fees. Registration may be upgraded to a higher number of users by paying the difference in cost.
Exemptions	The following are exempt from registration fees: students, if the teaching organization has paid for registration for at least one user; Australian Biological Resources Study (ABRS) staff and Flora and Fauna authors, if they are using the programs only for ABRS purposes. Exemption may also be granted in case of financial hardship.
Upgrades	Registration entitles you to use later versions of the programs, unless stated otherwise with the release of a new version.

DELTA Registration Form. 10 October 2000

Name:_____

Address:_____

_____

_____

_____

Country: _____   Fax:_____

Email: _____

Note. The programs and manuals are available for downloading at

http://biodiversity.uno.edu/delta/.

CSIRO Entomology does not supply disks or printed manuals.

Australia AU$

_____ Registration for all programs: single or first user AU$440

_____ Registration for all programs: additional users @ AU$110

TOTAL US$ _____

Other countries

_____ Registration for all programs: single or first user US$400

_____ Registration for all programs: additional users @ US$100

TOTAL _____

_____ I enclose a cheque (payable to CSIRO COLLECTOR OF MONEYS)

_____ Please debit my: Mastercard / Visa / Diners / Amex

Card number: _____ _____ _____ _____   Expiry date: ____/____

Signature: _____

Send to: DELTA, CSIRO Entomology

GPO Box 1700, Canberra ACT 2601, Australia

Fax +61 2 6246 4000 Email delta@ento.csiro.au

The Department of the Interior Mission

As the Nation's principal conservation agency, the Department of the Interior has responsibility for most of our nationally owned public lands and natural resources. This includes fostering sound use of our land and water resources; protecting our fish, wildlife, and biological diversity; preserving the environmental and cultural values of our national parks and historical places; and providing for the enjoyment of life through outdoor recreation. The Department assesses our energy and mineral resources and works to ensure that their development is in the best interests of all our people by encouraging stewardship and citizen participation in their care. The Department also has a major responsibility for American Indian reservation communities and for people who live in island territories under U.S. administration.

The Minerals Management Service Mission

As a bureau of the Department of the Interior, the Minerals Management Service's (MMS) primary responsibilities are to manage the mineral resources located on the Nation's Outer Continental Shelf (OCS), collect revenue from the Federal OCS and onshore Federal and Indian lands, and distribute those revenues.

Moreover, in working to meet its responsibilities, the **Offshore Minerals Management Program** administers the OCS competitive leasing program and oversees the safe and environmentally sound exploration and production of our Nation's offshore natural gas, oil and other mineral resources. The MMS **Minerals Revenue Management** meets its responsibilities by ensuring the efficient, timely and accurate collection and disbursement of revenue from mineral leasing and production due to Indian tribes and allottees, States and the U.S. Treasury.

The MMS strives to fulfill its responsibilities through the general guiding principles of: (1) being responsive to the public's concerns and interests by maintaining a dialogue with all potentially affected parties and (2) carrying out its programs with an emphasis on working to enhance the quality of life for all Americans by lending MMS assistance and expertise to economic development and environmental protection.